THE
INCAS

Peter Chrisp

Wayland

Look into the Past

Series editor: Joanna Bentley
Series designer: David West
Book designer: Joyce Chester

First published in 1994 by Wayland (Publishers) Limited,
61 Western Road, Hove, East Sussex, BN3 1JD, England

© Copyright 1994 Wayland (Publishers) Limited

British Library Cataloguing in Publication Data
  Chrisp, Peter
  Incas. – (Look into the Past series)
  I. Title   II. Series
  980.00498

ISBN 0 7502 1068 0

Typeset by Dorchester Typesetting Group Ltd., Dorset,
England.
Printed and bound in Italy by L.E.G.O. S.p.A., Vicenza.

Picture acknowledgements
The publishers wish to thank the following for providing the
photographs in this book: Archiv für Kunst und Geschichte,
Berlin 7 (both), 9 (both), 12; Bodleian Library, Oxford
(Mason. BB. 56. Vol. 6.) 28; E.T. Archive *cover*, 6 (bottom
Amano Museum, Lima), 8 (top Brunning Museum, Lima,
bottom Archaeological Museum, Lima), 13, 14 (University
Museum, Cuzco), 15 (both, right Archaeological Museum,
Lima), 16, 17 (top), 21 (bottom), 23 (bottom), 26; Werner
Forman Archive *cover*, 22 (Staatliche Museum, Berlin), 27
(top David Bernstein Fine Art, New York, bottom Museum
für Volkerkunde, Berlin), 29 (top British Museum); Nick
Saunders/ Barbara Heller 24, 25 (top); South American
Pictures/ Tony Morrison *cover*, 4, 6 (top), 10, 11 (both), 17
(bottom), 18, 19, 20, 22 (top), 25 (bottom), 29 (bottom);
South American Pictures/ Robert Francis 21 (top).
Map artwork by Jenny Hughes.

CONTENTS

Words that appear in **bold italic** in the text are explained in the glossary on page 30.

WHO WERE THE INCAS?

The Andes is the name of a range of high mountains stretching down the west coast of South America, through the countries of Ecuador, Peru, Bolivia and Chile. Five hundred years ago, there was an *empire* in the Andes, ruled by a people we call the Incas. In fact, the word Inca means 'lord' and it was the title of the rulers of the empire. They spoke a language called Quechua, which was really the proper name for the Inca people. Although the empire no longer exists, there are still six million Quechua speakers in the lands the Incas once ruled.

This is Machu ▶ Picchu, a ruined Inca town almost three kilometres above sea-level. Other Inca towns, such as Cuzco, are even higher. No other people in the world built towns as high up as the Incas. They were well suited to life in the mountains. The people had larger lungs than average, which helped them breathe in the thin mountain air.

The Inca empire ▶ was built up in less than a hundred years. This was thanks to the **conquests** of three great Inca rulers: Pachacuti, his son Topa Inca and Topa's son, Huayna Capac. By the time of Huayna Capac's death, around 1525, the Incas ruled over more than twelve million people, speaking at least twenty different languages. Their empire was more than 3,500 km long, linked up by 40,000 km of well-built roads.

The Incas called their empire 'Tahuantisuyu', which means 'The Land of the Four Quarters'. It was divided into four areas, or suyus, for each of the four directions. The centre was the capital, Cuzco. To the Incas, this was the centre of the world.

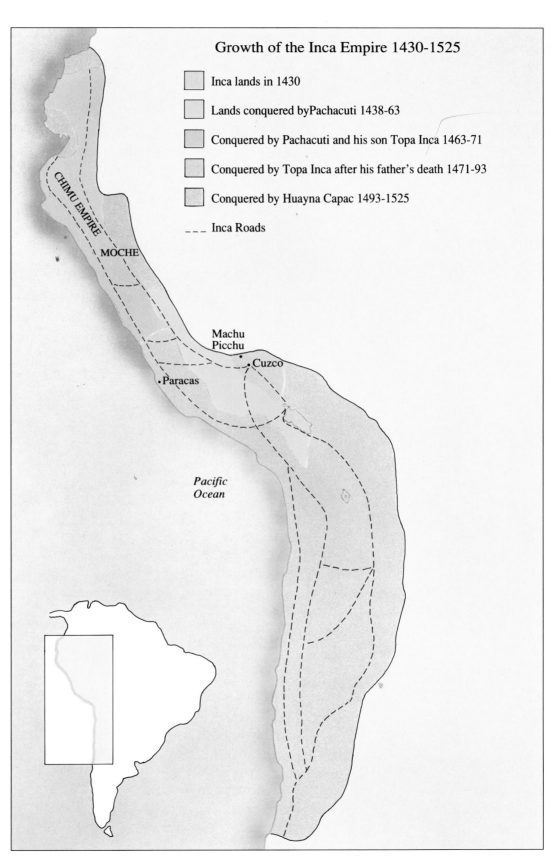

Growth of the Inca Empire 1430-1525

- Inca lands in 1430
- Lands conquered byPachacuti 1438-63
- Conquered by Pachacuti and his son Topa Inca 1463-71
- Conquered by Topa Inca after his father's death 1471-93
- Conquered by Huayna Capac 1493-1525
- - - - Inca Roads

CHIMU EMPIRE

MOCHE

Machu Picchu

•Cuzco

•Paracas

Pacific Ocean

5

BEFORE THE INCAS

Long before the time of the Incas, there were rich civilizations in the Andes. The Incas learned many things from these earlier peoples: how to weave cloth; how to build roads and bridges; and how to rule an empire. We know about the earlier peoples through objects found in their graves – pottery, gold ornaments and cloth.

▲ This piece of cloth was worn by a *mummy* found at Paracas, on the southern coast of Peru. It is more than two thousand years old, yet, thanks to the dry desert air, it is perfectly preserved. We know little about the Paracas people, apart from their great skill at weaving and *embroidery*. They decorated their cloth with pictures of animals, using 190 different shades of coloured cotton.

Between AD 100 and 900, another ▶ civilization grew up around the Moche valley on the northern coast. We know much more about the Moche (or Mochica) people, thanks to the fine pottery they buried with their dead. The pottery often shows scenes of ordinary life. The man on this pot is catching fish with a pelican. The pelican does the work but it is unable to swallow the fish because the man is holding it by the neck.

6

Warfare was very important to the Moche people. This is a prisoner who has been captured in a battle. He has been stripped and tied to a wooden frame. Even his ear plugs, worn as a sign of high rank, have been taken – you can see the holes in his ears. No wonder he looks unhappy!

The Incas treated their own prisoners of war just like this. No victory was complete until the defeated leaders had been **tortured** and killed. ▼

▲ Moche pottery is so skilfully made that it can show us what the people looked like. This is a portrait, probably of the person in whose tomb it was found.

◄ Some of the earlier people became powerful by conquering their neighbours, just as the Incas were to do. After AD 1000 a people called the Chimu conquered much of the north coast of Peru. The Chimu empire was well organized, with towns linked up by a network of roads, and official messengers carrying news. The Chimu were also fine craftspeople, especially in gold. Look at this head of a puma. Can you see its whiskers?

Unlike the Incas, ► who lived high in the mountains, the Chimu were a coastal people. They fished from boats made of tightly bound reeds, like the one on this piece of pottery. In Peru today, people still sail reed boats very like this one.

Here is another ▶ piece of Chimu gold, a strange animal which might be a cat or a sea monster.

The Chimu empire was itself conquered by the Incas in the 1460s. The Incas were so impressed by the Chimu gold work that they took all the Chimu craftspeople back to their capital, Cuzco, to work for them.

To the Incas, gold was an especially holy metal. Their chief god was the sun, and they called gold the 'sweat of the sun'. Silver was said to be the 'tears of the moon'. This is a gold death mask, worn by a Chimu king or noble. ▼

9

THE SAPA INCA

The ruler of the empire was called the Sapa Inca, or 'sole lord'. He claimed to be a child of the sun and he was treated as a god. When a Sapa Inca died, his body was preserved and he continued to 'live' in his palace. The dead Inca sat on a golden stool, watched over by a woman who whisked the flies away from his face. The dead rulers were served with food each day and, on special occasions, they were all carried out of their palaces so that they could feast together. Each new ruler had to build himself a new palace. By 1500 Cuzco was full of the palaces of dead Sapa Incas.

We know a lot about the lives of ▶ the Sapa Incas thanks to drawings made after the Incas had been conquered by the Spaniards in the 1530s. The artist, Felipe Huaman Poma, was the son of a Spanish conqueror and an Inca princess. This is his drawing of one of the last rulers, Manco Inca. He greets his chief nobles with a raised forefinger – the Inca salute. The nobles wear big ear plugs, which were signs of nobility. On his forehead, Manco has a red fringe, the Inca version of a crown. Manco and his men are getting ready for war.

The Sapa Inca and his Coya always travelled in a *litter*, sheltered under a covering of brightly coloured feathers. Look at the strange head-dresses of the men carrying the litter. The different peoples of the Inca Empire all had their own special head-dresses. These men are Carabaya people. Compare their head-dresses with the Lucana people carrying the litter on page 13. ▼

▲ This woman is a Coya, an Inca queen. Each Sapa Inca had many unofficial wives, and dozens of sons and daughters, who were the Inca nobility. Yet there was only one Coya and she was always the ruler's own sister. Like him, she was thought to be a child of the sun. By marrying his sister, the Sapa Inca made sure that their children only had the pure blood of the sun. This was important because one of their sons would be the next Sapa Inca.

Reyno lima xauxa chinchay coya

cleuan alguga los yis callaua ya-espauo apagearse

11

CONQUERING THE EMPIRE

The Incas were almost always successful in war, largely because of their great skill at organizing people and supplies. They could raise large armies and collect enough food to feed them for long periods. Using the Inca roads, these armies were able to travel quickly from place to place. As the empire grew, the Incas were able to raise even bigger armies from the conquered lands. The only full-time soldiers were the Sapa Inca's bodyguard and his relatives, who were the captains and generals. Most of the fighters were ordinary farmers, who were called up when they were needed.

Inca soldiers were armed with short wooden clubs, tipped with stone or bronze – like the one held by this Moche warrior. They protected themselves with a wooden helmet and a small shield made from wood or deerskin.

The Sapa Inca often led his troops in person. This is Huayna Capac, going into battle carried on a litter. He is hurling a stone with a sling – a weapon always used at the start of battles. All the men were expert slingers. As children, they practised by killing birds which came to feed on the crops.

llevan los y̅n̅s̅ andamarcas y
soras lucanas. parina cochas:
alaguerraybatalla depricesa
sa lo lleuan

◀ This is an Inca noble, dressed for war, painted on a wooden vase. His feathered helmet and spear are both signs of his rank as an officer. Inca nobles loved fighting. They trained for warfare from the age of fourteen and longed to prove their bravery and skill. Successful officers were rewarded with medals: these were silver badges which hung around their necks.

RULING THE EMPIRE

The Incas ruled over one of the best organized empires in history. They controlled the lives of everyone, through a system of officials. This system was like a triangle or pyramid: at the bottom were millions of ordinary farmers; above them were thousands of officials and hundreds of higher officials; and above them there were the four *governors* of the quarters of the empire. At the very top of the pyramid was the Sapa Inca.

People had to spend part of each year working for the state – mining, building roads or serving in the army. Throughout the empire, there were great storehouses where food was kept. The Incas made sure that no one starved. In return, everyone was expected to work.

Although the Incas ▶ had no writing system, they could keep records using lengths of knotted string called *quipus*. The colour of the string stood for whatever was being counted – for example, red string for warriors and yellow string for gold or maize. The knots stood for numbers. This is a quipu keeper, an official trained to understand the quipus. Quipus helped the Inca rulers to organize their empire – to raise armies and gather workers for building schemes, and to collect enough food to feed them.

▲ You can see different sizes and types of knot on this quipu. A simple knot stands for one. Longer knots show numbers up to nine (like us, the Incas counted in tens). At the bottom of the string, the knots stand for units (ones). Higher up, they stand for tens, then hundreds, then thousands.

15

News was delivered very fast in the Inca empire by official messengers. They lived in huts placed every two kilometres along the roads. A messenger would run at great speed from his own hut to the next one, where another messenger would take the message on. This system meant that important news could travel 250 km in one day. A messenger had to be a fast runner and have a good memory – messages had to be learned by heart as quickly as possible. This runner is blowing a note on a conch shell, to let the next messenger know he is approaching. In his left hand, he holds a club and a sling, for self-defence, and a basket holding a quipu. He could be seen in the distance, because he wore a head-dress of white feathers.

There are many ▶ deep gorges and fast rivers in the Andes. The Inca roads crossed them using strong rope bridges. These were regularly checked by officials and replaced when the rope became worn. The man on the left of this picture is an inspector of bridges. His headband and big ear plugs show that he is an Inca noble.

These are llamas, animals distantly related to camels. Like camels, llamas are useful because they can go without food or water for days. The Incas kept great herds of llamas to carry loads of food and other goods along the roads – to feed the armies and workers and to fill the storehouses. Llamas were also useful in providing wool, meat and dung, which was burned as fuel. ▼

GODS

The Incas believed in a great god called Viracocha, who had made the world. Apart from Viracocha, who was invisible, the Inca gods could all be seen or felt. The most important was Inti, the sun, who was believed to be the father of the Sapa Inca and protector of the Inca people. Like the Sapa Inca, he was married to his own sister, Mama Quilla, the moon. Other gods included Pacha Mama, the earth, and Illapa, thunder and lightning.

◄ This is an Inti Huatana, which means 'post where the sun is tied'. It was used to keep track of the sun's yearly movements. In the winter, for example, the sun sinks lower and lower in the sky. Eventually it reaches a point, called a solstice, when it stops sinking and starts to rise again. The Incas knew when the solstice was due by looking at the shadow cast by this post. This was the signal for religious **ceremonies** to make the sun come back, to warm the lands of the Incas. There were great celebrations when the sun started to rise again.

▲ As well as worshipping the great gods like Inti, the Incas worshipped huacas, which were holy places or things. Huacas included rocks, springs, caves, mountains, rivers and unusually shaped trees. All of these were thought to have special powers and the Incas made offerings to them to ask for their help. Less important huacas were offered maize beer. The more powerful huacas were offered **sacrifices**: children and llamas were killed and buried beside them. These important huacas had their own priests and priestesses who looked after them. This huaca is a holy spring at Tambo Machay, near Cuzco. The Incas channelled the water into a pool in the foreground.

coropo napampa saynam.

Throughout the year, there were many *festivals* in honour of the gods. Some were held to mark important events in the farming year, such as the harvesting of crops. Others marked big events in the lives of the people, such as the coming of age of the young Incas. During the festivals, people feasted, drank beer and danced. Here you can see the women singing and beating on drums. The men, dressed as birds, are getting ready to dance.

20

FARMING

The mountains of the Andes are not easy places to grow food. Long periods without rain, poor soil, bad frosts and steep slopes all make farming difficult. The Incas found answers to all these problems, thanks to their great skill at organizing people.

◄ The problem of steep slopes and poor soil was solved by building flat raised strips called terraces. These were made by building long stone walls and then piling up soil from the valleys behind them. The soil was made *fertile* with sea bird droppings. These terraces, at Pisac, were planned by professional Inca *architects*.

Lack of water was solved by building stone ► *reservoirs* to store the rain until it was needed. The Incas also made stone-lined *irrigation* channels, carrying water from rivers and mountain streams to the tops of the terraces. It was then channelled down the hillside through the crops. In the cold, higher terraces the Incas grew potatoes, which stand up well to frost. Lower down they grew maize. This woman is opening an irrigation channel to water the growing maize plants.

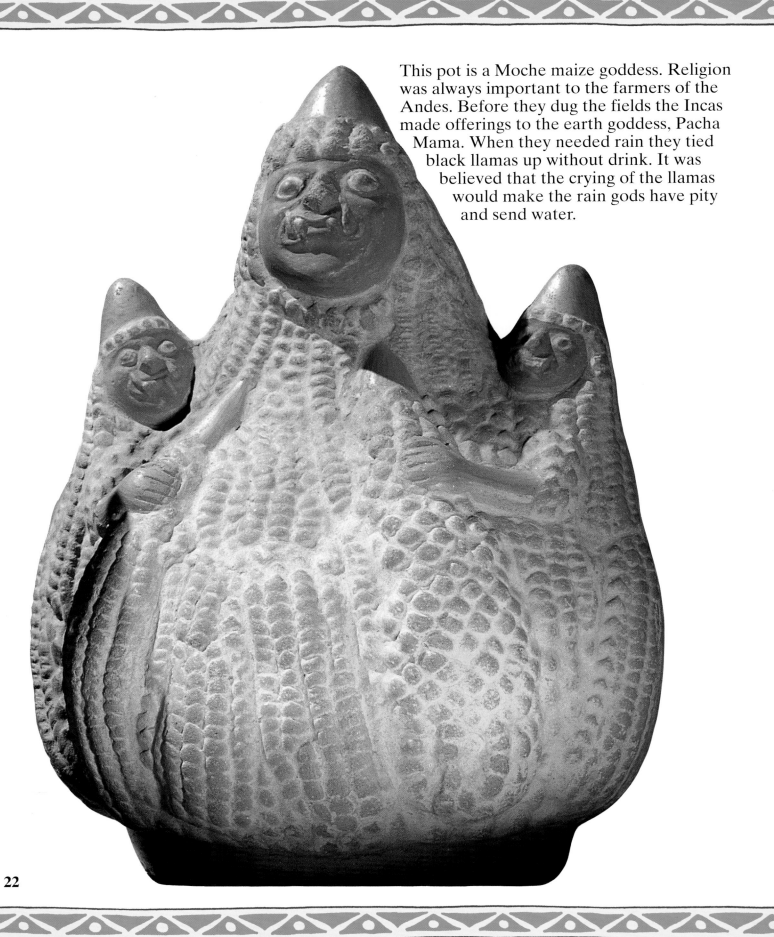

This pot is a Moche maize goddess. Religion was always important to the farmers of the Andes. Before they dug the fields the Incas made offerings to the earth goddess, Pacha Mama. When they needed rain they tied black llamas up without drink. It was believed that the crying of the llamas would make the rain gods have pity and send water.

◀ This piece of wood, carved and painted like the head of a puma, is a drinking cup. It would have been used to drink beer made from maize. Everyone, from the Sapa Inca down to the poorest farmer, drank this beer, called chicha. It was made by old women who chewed the grains of maize and then spat them into jars of warm water. This process made the maize break down, producing alcohol. Eight days later it was ready for drinking.

Men and women worked together in the ▶ fields. The men dug into the soil with long wooden foot ploughs, called tacclas. The women crouched in front of them, breaking up the earth with their hands. This drawing shows the Sapa Inca himself digging, watched over by his father, the sun god. This was a religious ceremony to make sure of a good harvest. The Sapa Inca is on the far left. On the right his Coya brings him a golden cup filled with maize beer, so that he can drink a toast to the sun. The men and women sing as they work.

23

BUILDING

The Incas were wonderful builders with stone. Using only bronze chisels and stone hammers, they cut enormous blocks into different shapes and sizes, fitting them together like pieces in a jigsaw. This method made Inca walls much stronger than any built nowadays. In 1950 two-thirds of Cuzco was wrecked in a terrible earthquake. But not one of the old Inca walls collapsed.

It was said to have taken seventy-five years to build this fortress, Sacsahuaman, overlooking Cuzco. Twenty thousand men worked on it. Four thousand of them worked in the *quarries*, cutting the stones. Six thousand men dragged the stones on wooden rollers to the site. Here ten thousand men were kept busy, building earth ramps to raise the blocks; dragging the blocks up the ramps; and then shaping them and fitting them into place. Some of these stones are over six metres high and weigh over a hundred tonnes.

A doorway from ▶ the same fortress gives you a closer view of the stone blocks. They fit so tightly that it is impossible to slip a knife blade between them. Inca doorways and windows were always wide at the bottom and narrow at the top. This made them strong.

This aerial view of Machu Picchu shows you the size of Inca building schemes. On the right, you can see the houses and temples. On the left, there are the great terraces for farming. Machu Picchu is the most famous Inca site because it is so well preserved. It was abandoned by the Incas for some unknown reason and only rediscovered in 1911. ▼

WEAVING

It was the women who made the Inca clothes, using cotton and wool – especially the fine wool of the alpaca, a smaller relative of the llama. Llama wool, which was coarser, was used for blankets. The first stage was colouring the wool, using dyes from plants and shellfish. Then it was spun by hand into fine thread. Finally, it was woven into lengths of cloth on a loom.

◄ This woman is weaving cloth using a backstrap loom. One end is strapped around her back while the other end is tied to a tree. She passes the coloured thread from side to side, weaving it in between the lengthwise threads. In South America today, women still weave cloth like this.

Some Inca tunics ► have survived, showing us just what skilled weavers the women were. Look at the complicated patterns in the small boxes and the flowers and animals on the white tunic. You can see a tunic just like this in the drawing by Felipe Huaman Poma on page 23.

This hat, worn by ▶
an Inca noble, has
been carefully woven
and then decorated
with feathers.
Compare it with the
hat worn by the noble
in the painting on
page 29.

THE FALL OF THE INCAS

The Inca Empire fell apart in a very short time, soon after the death of the great ruler Huayna Capac in 1525. Two of his sons – Atahuallpa and Huascar – quarrelled over which of them should be the next Sapa Inca. They fought a bloody war against each other, which ended in Atahuallpa's victory in 1532. While the war was still going on news came that strange people had arrived on the coast. Everything about these visitors seemed odd – they dressed in metal suits, rode on unknown animals (horses) and they had hair growing out of their chins. They were Spaniards, warlike people who had recently arrived in the Americas. Atahuallpa was curious to see them and, after his victory, he invited them to visit him. There were less than two hundred of them, so he felt no reason to be afraid of them.

This picture shows ▶ what happened next. Without warning, the Spaniards fired their cannon and charged at the Inca's army. Cutting down all the warriors who tried to protect Atahuallpa, the Spaniards took him prisoner. The Spaniards promised Atahuallpa his freedom in exchange for a huge ransom in gold. The Inca paid the ransom, but instead of freeing him, they killed him.

This painted ▶ wooden jar shows us an Inca view of the Spaniards and the Africans they brought with them. An Inca noble walks behind a Spanish trumpeter and an African drummer.

Spanish rule brought many changes to life in the Andes. The Inca religion was stamped out and people were forced to become **Christians**. The Spaniards did not understand the Inca farming system and the irrigation canals were left to crumble. Millions of people died from diseases, like smallpox, brought from Europe.

◀ Despite the destruction of the Inca empire, many things about ordinary life have not changed in the Andes. Today, people still spin and weave wool in the old way. They still use llamas to carry their goods. They still dress up in colourful costumes and dance to celebrate festivals.

29

GLOSSARY

Architects People who design buildings.

Ceremonies Formal acts, such as religious celebrations.

Christians Followers of the teachings of Jesus Christ.

Civilization A particular group of people and the way that they live.

Conquests Winning battles and taking over other people's lands.

Embroidery Decorative needlework which makes a picture or a pattern.

Empire A large area of land, including different peoples, ruled by a single state.

Fertile Able to create new life. Fertile fields are those which are good for the growing of plants.

Festival A celebration, like a big party, to mark an important event.

Governors People who rule areas of a country.

Irrigation The science of storing and directing water for farming.

Litter A chair carried on poles used as transport by the Sapa Inca and his family. Everyone else had to walk – the Incas had no animals big enough to ride and they knew nothing about the wheel.

Mummy A preserved dead body. Dead Sapa Incas were made into mummies, which were then treated with all the honours given to the living ruler.

Quarries Open mines where stones are cut or dug up.

Quipus Lengths of knotted string used to record information. Quipus were said to be used by the Incas to record their history, but no one knows how this was done.

Reservoir A big artificial pool or container made for storing large amounts of water.

Sacrifices Killing people or animals to offer to a god or goddess.

Tortured Made to suffer extreme pain.

IMPORTANT DATES

400 BC – Paracas people, on the southern coast of Peru, make fine weaving.
AD 100-900 – The Moche civilization grows on the northern coast of Peru.
1000-1460s – Chimu people conquer an empire on the northern coast of Peru.
1200-1300 – The Incas settle in the Cuzco valley.
1438-63 – Pachacuti Inca conquers the people to the west of Cuzco.
1463-71 – Pachacuti and his son Topa Inca conquer the Chimu empire.

1471-93 – Topa Inca conquers the southern part of the empire, now part of Chile.
1492 – Spanish ships, captained by Columbus, first reach the Americas.
1493-1525 – Huayna Capac conquers more lands in the north.
1525-32 – War between Huayna Capac's sons, Atahuallpa and Huascar.
1532 – Spaniards, led by Francisco Pizarro, capture Atahuallpa.
1536 – Manco Inca leads an unsuccessful rising against the Spaniards.

PRONUNCIATION

Many of the Inca names look difficult. It helps if you remember that 'Hua' sounds like 'wa' and 'qui' sounds like 'kee'. So 'quipu' sounds like 'kee-poo'; 'Huaca' is 'waka', and 'Tahuantisuyu' is 'Ta-wan-tee-soo-yoo'.

BOOKS TO READ

An Inca Farmer by Marion Morrison (Wayland, 1986)
This gives an introduction to the Inca empire, as well as an insight into the lifestyles of ordinary people.

The Incas by Sarita Kendall (Heinemann Children's Reference, 1991)
This book uses archaeological evidence to draw up a picture of the life of the Incas.

Incas, Myths and Legends by Frances Halton (Cherrytree Books, 1991)
Some of the exciting stories from Inca myths are told here, with beautiful illustrations.

Ancient America: Cultural Atlas for Young People by Marion Wood (Facts on File, 1990)
This includes a lot of information about the Incas, and the peoples of Peru, such as the Moche, who lived before them.

INDEX